LIFE STYLE
A Workbook

HAROLD H. MOSAK, PhD
SEYMOUR SCHNEIDER, EdD
and
LISA E. MOSAK

Table of Contents

PREFACE

The art of interpreting life styles is a complex one. It is not truly learned through attending a class on life style or through observation of an experienced life style interpreter "plying his trade." Reading a book and then jumping in and "getting one's feet wet" only succeeds in foisting incompetent interpreters and misleading interpretations upon an unsuspecting public. Since practicing beyond the level of one's professional competence is regarded by professional associations as unethical, such practice should be avoided. Incorrect life style interpretation may damage a person, and the student is well-advised to heed the caution given all medical students – *primum non nocere*! (First, do no harm!)

It is with these cautions that this workbook is presented. Filling in blanks will not make of the student an experienced interpreter. The latter is only accomplished by doing many such data analyses under the supervision of an experienced teacher or practitioner. However, the workbook will provide the student with an opportunity to hone his/her skills, to gain some practice without potentially jeopardizing the welfare of others, and to receive some feedback about "guessing" from the answers provided in the back of the book.

The problems in this workbook were designed to be representative of the more common problems encountered in life style interpretation. We attempted to avoid unique and tricky problems. The answers represent **a sampling** of the kinds of guesses which might be made from the data. Experienced interpreters, and even some less-experienced one, will undoubtedly make additional guesses.

The workbook is intended for use in a one- or two-term class, but it may also be used profitably in independent study. For a rationale for the understanding of the procedures taught in this workbook, please consult Shulman, B. H. and Mosak, H. H. (1988), *A Manual for life style assessment*, Muncie, IN: Accelerated Development.

In our effort to find names to use in this workbook, we have sometimes used those of some of our Adlerian friends and colleagues. The names were used randomly and in no way bear any association to the given example.

We are deeply appreciative of Judy Weigel's devotion to this project in the preparation of this manuscript.

March 17, 1980

HAROLD H. MOSAK, Ph.D.
SEYMOUR SCHNEIDER, Ed.D.
LISA E. MOSAK

CONTENTS

UNIT 1
SIBLING CONSTELLATION I

What guesses might you make about the following clients? [*Client's name is italicized and **bold.***]

1. Bea +9, Wyn +8, Phil +7, ***Gary*** 20

   a. ______________________________

   ____

   b. ______________________________

   ____

   c. ______________________________

   ____

   d. ______________________________

   ____

2. Donna +3, Marguerite +2, ***Harry*** 26, Barbara -1

   a. ______________________________

   ____

   b. ______________________________

   ____

   c. ______________________________

   ____

   d. ______________________________

   ____

3. Alex [+3] (deceased), ***Lenore*** 24, Gene -4

   a. ______________________________

   ____

   b. ______________________________

   ____

   c. ______________________________

   ____

d. ______________________________

____

4. ***Marlene*** 38, Howard -2, Nick -3, Norman -4

a. ______________________________

____

b. ______________________________

____

c. ______________________________

____

d. ______________________________

____

5. Guy +12, Ernie +10, Dennis +8, ***Duane*** 46

a. ______________________________

____

b. ______________________________

____

c. ______________________________

____

d. ______________________________

____

6. Milton [+8], Dan [+6], Herb [+3], ***Jack*** 16

a. ______________________________

____

b. ______________________________

____

c. ______________________________

____

d. ______________________________

____

7. Lawrence +3, Alfred +2, ***Janice*** 43, Edgar -2

a. ______________________________

____

b. ______________________________

____

c. ______________________________

____

d. ______________________________

____

8. Lorraine +3, Hy +2, ***Audrey*** 18

a. ______________________________

____

b. ______________________________

____

c. ______________________________

____

d. ______________________________

____

9. ***Sherwin*** 21

a. ______________________________

____

b. ______________________________

____

c. ______________________________

____

d. ____

____

10. Mort +5, Ned+3, Andrew +2, ***Sheila*** 66

a. ____

____

b. ____

____

c. ____

____

d. ____

____

11. ***Herman*** 34, Eunice -2, Beverly -3, Joyce -4

a. ____

____

b. ____

____

c. ____

____

d. ____

____

UNIT 2
SIBLING CONSTELLATION II

1. Tom is ten years older than his brother John.

   What is the family position for each brother?

   ____

   ____

   Some possible roles for Tom with respect to John are:

   a. ____

   b. ____

   c. ____

2. Mary and Sue are sisters. They are the same age, but they are not twins. Some possible explanations are:

   a. ____

   b. ____

   c. ____

3. Bill is the oldest child. He was born many years after his parents' marriage.

   a. His role may be that of ______________________________

   His parents may engage in the following kinds of behavior:

   b. ____

   c. ____

   Bill's self concept may include such statements as:

   d. ____

   e. ____

   f. ____

   His view of other people may include such statements as:

   g. ____

   h. ____

4. The sibling distribution is Boy, Girl, Girl, Girl (BGGG).

   Briefly describe the most likely roles for B.

   a. ______________________________

   Describe another possible role in a family where the girls are highly valued.

   b. ______________________________

5. Given the sibling distribution GGGGB, what are most likely roles for B?

   a. ______________________________

   b. ______________________________

   Describe the manner in which his sisters might treat him.

   c. ______________________________

   Describe the view of women that he may adopt later in life.

   d. ______________________________

   e. ______________________________

6. Given the sibling distribution BBBG, what are the most likely roles for G?

   a. ______________________________

   b. ______________________________

   c. ______________________________

   Describe the manner in which her brothers might treat her.

   d. ______________________________

   e. ______________________________

   f. ______________________________

   Describe the view of men that she may adopt later in life.

   g. ______________________________

   h. ______________________________

UNIT 3
SIBLING DESCRIPTIONS

What guesses can you make from the following data?

1.

John +2	***Mary 31***	Tom -1
Smart	Did poorly in school	Got straight "A"s

a. ____

b. ____

c. ____

d. ____

2.

Bill 47	Sue -2
Not outgoing Better in school Athletic Liked tinkering Always fighting	More outgoing Average in school Very musical

a. ____

b. ____

c. ____

d. ____

3.

Paul +3	***Joan 54***	Bob -2
Always in fights Liked sports	Didn't like teachers telling her what to do Tomboy Better than Bob in sports	Mama's boy Really stubborn Often called "sissy"

a. ____

____

b. ____

____

c. ____

____

d. ____

____

4.

John +5	Frank +4	***Cliff 20***
A great guy He took me everywhere Taught me to do things	Protected me in fights Gave me extra money Good in sports	Spoiled brat Loved sports Got my own way a lot

a. ______________________________

b. ______________________________

c. ______________________________

5.

Phyllis +3	***Willa 16***	Lila -8
Always did the right thing Never in trouble	Always fighting with Phyllis Misbehaved in school	Everyone's darling Very sweet, cute, good Smart We took care of her Father's favorite

a. ______________________________

____

b. ______________________________

____

c. ______________________________

____

d. ______________________________

____

e. ______________________________

____

f. ______________________________

____

g. ______________________________

____

UNIT 4
SIBLING GROUPING

Divide the following sibling constellations into subgroups.

Example:

Lucy +3, ***Claire*** *54*, Roberta -9

a. This is a *2-1* family.

b. Claire is the *younger of two girls*.

---

1. ***Renee*** 63, Sally -2, Simon -5, Walter -7

   a. This is probably a ____________________________ family.

   b. The division is probably upon the basis of

   ______________________________ and ______________________________

   c. Renee is the __________________________________

   d. Simon is the __________________________________

2. Virginia +7, ***Sally*** 34, Carolyn -2

   Sally played and fought with Carolyn.

   Sally is probably the _______________________________

3. Marilyn+3, Joyce+1½, ***Linda*** 15

   Linda played with Marilyn and fought with Joyce.

   This is probably a __________________________ family.

4. Jane has two older brothers and two brothers younger than herself. The most likely roles for Jane are:

   a. ____

   b. ____

Jane's convictions may include such statements as:

   c. ____

   d. ____

If this constellation groups itself into groups of 2-3, Jane will be the oldest of the younger group. In this group Jane may play such roles as:

e. ______________________________

f. ______________________________

g. ______________________________

If the family constellation is divided into a 3-2 grouping, Jane will be the youngest of the older group. In this position she may:

h. ______________________________

____

5. John +10, Mary +8, ***Susan*** 36, Paul -2, James -3

a. This is a ____________________ family.

b. Susan is ____________________

c. Mary and James are ____________________

d. Susan may have found her place by ____________________

e. Susan may have also found her place by

____

____

6. Tom +13, George +11, ***Bob*** 20

a. George is ______________________________

b. Bob is ______________________________

c. Tom and George may serve as ____________________

7. Maxine+17, ***Arthur*** 30, Joe-2

   a. Arthur is ____

   b. Maxine is ____

   c. Maxine may have ____

   d. Maxine may have ____

8. Eugene [+3], ***Mitchell*** 24, Teddy -2 (male)

   Eugene died when he was 10 years old.

   a. This is a ___________________________ family.

   b. Mitchell's position in the family was probably _____________________

   ____

9. Gil [+2], two miscarriages, ***Gus*** 26

   Gil died before Gus was born.

   a. Gus' position in the family may be that of _______________________

   b. Gus may be the younger of two if _____________________________

   c. Gus' parents probably ___________________________________

UNIT 5
CHILDHOOD ILLNESSES

What guesses could you make if given the following information?

1. Bernard almost died of an infection/fever at age 4.

   a. ____________________

   b. ____________________

   c. ____________________

   d. ____________________

2. Ron was knocked unconscious by getting hit with a baseball bat at age 8.

   a. ____________________

   b. ____________________

   c. ____________________

   d. ____________________

3. Leo always had cuts and bruises.

   a. ____________________

   b. ____________________

   c. ____________________

   d. ____________________

4. Dorothy was sickly with asthma and rashes. She missed many days of school.

   a. ____________________

   b. ____________________

   c. ____________________

   d. ____________________

   e. ____________________

UNIT 6
CHILDHOOD TALENTS

What guesses could you make about the client given the following information?

1. Mike +3, ***Ted*** 30, Eva -2

   Mike was on a quiz show representing his second grade class.

   a. ______________________________

   b. ______________________________

   c. ______________________________

   d. ______________________________

   e. ______________________________

2. ***Lisa*** 30, Ellen -2, Toby -1

   Lisa modeled children's clothes for national magazines.

   a. ______________________________

   b. ______________________________

   c. ______________________________

   d. ______________________________

   e. ______________________________

   f. ______________________________

   g. ______________________________

3. Walter +3, Beth +2, ***Phil*** 45

   Walter and Beth both played in school bands.

   a. ______________________________

   b. ______________________________

   c. ______________________________

4. Upon being pressed by the examiner Richard replies, "Nothing really. I was first in my class and broke the Little League record for most base hits.

   a. ______________________________

   b. ______________________________

   c. ______________________________

   d. ______________________________

   e. ______________________________

   f. ______________________________

   g. ______________________________

5. Edna +5, ***Shirley*** 37

   "Who cares? My parents didn't even come when I was the lead in all my school plays."

   a. ______________________________

   b. ______________________________

   c. ______________________________

   d. ______________________________

   e. ______________________________

   f. ______________________________

   g. ______________________________

UNIT 7
CHILDHOOD FEARS

What implications would you draw about the client if he says the following?

1. "I was afraid of water and walking over bridges."

   a. ____

   b. ____

2. "I was afraid of my parents dying."

   a. ____

   b. ____

   c. ____

   d. ____

3. "I was afraid of my parents fighting."

   a. ____

   b. ____

   c. ____

   d. ____

4. "I was afraid of getting hit by Father."

   a. ____

   b. ____

   c. ____

   d. ____

5. "I was afraid of shadows on my bedroom wall at night. They looked like monsters."

   a. ______________________________

   b. ______________________________

   c. ______________________________

   d. ______________________________

6. "I was afraid of exams and reading in front of the class."

   a. ______________________________

   b. ______________________________

   c. ______________________________

   d. ______________________________

   e. ______________________________

   f. ______________________________

   g. ______________________________

7. "I was afraid of wetting my pants at school."

   a. ______________________________

   b. ______________________________

   c. ______________________________

8. "I was afraid of tigers chasing me in my dreams."

   a. ______________________________

9. "I was afraid of falling in my dreams."

   a. ______________________________

   b. ______________________________

   c. ______________________________

10. "I was afraid of getting dirty, and I still am."

    a. ______________________________

    b. ______________________________

    c. ______________________________

    d. ______________________________

UNIT 8
CHILDHOOD AMBITIONS

What guesses might you make about the following childhood ambitions?

1. Nurse or doctor

    a. ______________________________

    b. ______________________________

    c. ______________________________

2. Doctor or lawyer

    a. ______________________________

    b. ______________________________

    c. ______________________________

3. Priest or nun

    a. ______________________________

    b. ______________________________

    c.. ______________________________

    d. ______________________________

    e. ______________________________

    f. ______________________________

4. Pilot

    a. ______________________________

    b. ______________________________

    c. ______________________________

    d. ______________________________

5. Movie star
   a. ____________________
   b. ____________________
   c. ____________________
   d. ____________________

6. Wife and mother
   a. ____________________
   b. ____________________
   c. ____________________

7. Right fielder
   a. ____________________
   b. ____________________

8. Acrobat
   a. ____________________
   b. ____________________
   c. ____________________

9. Government worker or work for the county or state
   a. ____________________
   b. ____________________

10. Police officer
   a. ____________________
   b. ____________________
   c. ____________________

UNIT 9
TRAITS – MANNER OF RESPONDING

In gathering the trait ratings, what might you surmise if the client...

1. *continually answers, "I don't know?"*

    a. ______________________________

    b. ______________________________

    c.. ______________________________

    d. ______________________________

    e. ______________________________

    f. ______________________________

    g. ______________________________

    h. ______________________________

2. *takes five minutes deciding how to rate each trait?*

    a. ______________________________

    b. ______________________________

    c.. ______________________________

    d. ______________________________

    e. ______________________________

    f. ______________________________

3. *lists most or all of the traits as "average" for him/herself?*

    a. ______________________________

    b. ______________________________

c. ____

d. ____

e. ____

f. ____

g. ____

4. *does not rate, but gives you examples of what the siblings did as kids?*

a. ____

b. ____

c.. ____

d. ____

e. ____

f. ____

UNIT 10
TRAIT MEANINGS

Since Adlerian psychology stresses use rather than possession, Adlerians generally avoid the use of descriptive terms and translate them into "movement" terms. For example, "Arthur is dependent" can be translated as "Arthur puts others into his service."

Translate the following into "movement" terms:

1. Betty is shy.

   ____

   ____

2. Charles is stubborn.

   ____

   ____

3. Don is vain.

   ____

   ____

4. Edith is a charmer.

   ____

   ____

5. Frank is comforting.

   ____

   ____

6. Gail is sensitive and easily hurt.

   ____

   ____

7. Hank is bossy.

____

____

8. Jane has a temper.

____

____

9. Kurt has high standards of right and wrong.

____

____

UNIT 11
TRAIT CLUSTERS

List some possible conclusions you might make from the following constellations of traits.

1. **Bert**: Intelligence – high
   Grades – low

a. __________

b. __________

c. __________

d __________

e. __________

f. __________

g. __________

h __________

i. __________

j. __________

k __________

l. __________

2. **Tony**: Demanded own way – high
   Got own way – low

a. __________

b. __________

c. __________

d __________

e. __________

f. __________

3. **Vicki**: Critical of others – high
Critical of self – high

a. ______________________________

b. ______________________________

c. ______________________________

d ______________________________

e. ______________________________

f. ______________________________

4. **Althea**: Critical of others – high
Critical of self – low

a. ______________________________

b. ______________________________

c. ______________________________

d ______________________________

e. ______________________________

f. ______________________________

5. **Doris**: Critical of others – low
Critical of self – high

a. ______________________________

b. ______________________________

c. ______________________________

d ______________________________

e. ______________________________

f. ______________________________

g. ______________________________

h. ______________________________

i. ______________________________

6. **Ken**: Critical of others – low
Critical of self – low

a. ______

b. ______

c. ______

d ______

e. ______

7. **Dwayne**: Considerate – high
Bossy – high

a. ______

b. ______

c. ______

d ______

8. **Margaret**: Considerate – low
Bossy – high

a. ______

b. ______

c. ______

9. **Rosemary**: Considerate – high
Bossy – low

a. ______

b. ______

c. ______

d ______

e. ______

10. **Leon**:	Rebellious	–	high
	Bossy	–	high
	Demanded own way	–	high
	Temper	–	high

a. ____________________

b. ____________________

c. ____________________

d ____________________

11. **Martha**:	Rebellious	–	high
	Charming	–	high
	Pleasing	–	high
	Bossy	–	high
	Demanded own way	–	high
	Temper	–	high

a. ____________________

b. ____________________

12. **Bertha**:	Stubborn	–	high
	Sulked	–	high
	Shy	–	high
	Sensitive	–	high

a. ____________________

13. **Zach**:	Mischief	–	low
	Rebellion	–	low
	Punished	–	high

a. ____________________

b. ____________________

c. ____________________

d ____________________

14. **Earl**:

Mischief	–	low
Rebellion	–	low
Punished	–	high

a. ______________________________

b. ______________________________

c. ______________________________

d ______________________________

e. ______________________________

15. **Jane**:

Demanded own way	–	low
Temper	–	high

a. ______________________________

b. ______________________________

c. ______________________________

16. **Roz**:

Stubborn	–	low
Fighter	–	high

a. ______________________________

b. ______________________________

c. ______________________________

17. **Aaron**:

Stubborn	–	high
Fighter	–	low

a. ______________________________

b. ______________________________

c. ______________________________

18. **Mildred**:

Feminine	–	high
Masculine	–	high

a. ______________________________

b. ______________________________

c. ______________________________

19. **Joy**: Sociable – high
Shy – high

a. ______________________________

b. ______________________________

c. ______________________________

20. **Abe**: Got own way – high
Sulked – high
Sensitive – high

a. ______________________________

b. ______________________________

21. **Jerome**: Standards of right and wrong – high
Critical of others – high
Idealistic – high

a. ______________________________

b. ______________________________

c. ______________________________

UNIT 12
PHYSICAL DEVELOPMENT

On the basis of the following information, what are some conclusions you might draw?

1. Harriet was the only one in her family to have flaming red hair.

   a. ______________________________

   b. ______________________________

   c. ______________________________

   d ______________________________

2. Tony was small and weak but a fighter.

   a. ______________________________

   b. ______________________________

3. Marty was poor in sports. He was often the last one picked for the team.

   a. ______________________________

   b. ______________________________

   c. ______________________________

   d ______________________________

4. Marv was overweight.

   a. ______________________________

   b. ______________________________

   c. ______________________________

   d ______________________________

   e. ______________________________

   f. ______________________________

   g. ______________________________

5. Ann was skinny and underweight.

a. ______

b. ______

c. ______

d ______

e. ______

f. ______

6. Pam was always the largest girl in the group.

a. ______

b. ______

c. ______

d ______

e. ______

f. ______

g. ______

7. Evan had buck teeth and the kids called him "Beaver."

a. ______

b. ______

c. ______

d. ______

UNIT 13
SCHOOL INFORMATION

What are possible conclusions might you draw on the basis of the following information?

1. Steve says his parents didn't pay much attention to his report cards.

   a. ______________________________

   b. ______________________________

   c. ______________________________

   d ______________________________

2. Neal didn't get along with his teachers.

   a. ______________________________

   b. ______________________________

   c. ______________________________

   d ______________________________

   e. ______________________________

3. Eva was often the teacher's pet.

   a. ______________________________

   b. ______________________________

   c. ______________________________

   d ______________________________

4. Stuart was poor in spelling but good in math.

   a. ______________________________

   b. ______________________________

   c. ______________________________

   d ______________________________

5. Jerry was very poor in reading.

a. ______________________________

b. ______________________________

c. ______________________________

6. Sadie was good in spelling and poor in penmanship.

a. ______________________________

b. ______________________________

c. ______________________________

7. Sam disliked math but was good in it.

a. ______________________________

b. ______________________________

c. ______________________________

8. Judy liked art but didn't do well in spelling.

a. ______________________________

b. ______________________________

c. ______________________________

d. ______________________________

9. Mel's favorite school subjects were gym and recess.

a. ______________________________

b. ______________________________

c. ______________________________

d ______________________________

e. ______________________________

10. Jane was conforming but poor in spelling.

    a. ______________________________

    b. ______________________________

    c. ______________________________

11. Dave was obedient but poor in penmanship.

    a. ______________________________

    b. ______________________________

    c. ______________________________

    d. ______________________________

12. Rose attended Catholic school.

    a. ______________________________

    b. ______________________________

    c. ______________________________

    d. ______________________________

UNIT 14
SOCIAL INFORMATION

What conclusions might you draw from the following information?

1. Hy had few friends.

   a. ____________________

   b. ____________________

   c. ____________________

   d ____________________

   e. ____________________

   f. ____________________

   g. ____________________

   h. ____________________

2. Leah had many friends but never had a best friend.

   a. ____________________

   b. ____________________

   c. ____________________

3. Joan played with children of whom her parents disapproved.

   a. ____________________

   b. ____________________

   c. ____________________

   d ____________________

   e. ____________________

4. Jack was always the leader in his group.

   a. ______________________________

   b. ______________________________

   c. ______________________________

   d ______________________________

5. Elaine was part of her group but she was afraid of being the leader.

   a. ______________________________

   b. ______________________________

   c. ______________________________

6. Irwin was the clown of the group.

   a. ______________________________

   b. ______________________________

   c. ______________________________

UNIT 15
SEXUAL INFORMATION

What possible interpretations might you place on the following data?

1. Faye states, "You could never talk about sex in my family."

   a. ______________________________

   b. ______________________________

   c. ______________________________

   d ______________________________

   e. ______________________________

2. Nathan reports, "I couldn't ever imagine doing it [sex]. It was a long way off."

   a. ______________________________

   b. ______________________________

   c. ______________________________

   d ______________________________

   e. ______________________________

3. Beverly states, "I hated getting my period. It was a curse every month."

   a. ______________________________

   b. ______________________________

   c. ______________________________

   d ______________________________

   e. ______________________________

   f. ______________________________

   g. ______________________________

4. Wendy says, "I was self-conscious when I got my first bra."

a. ______________________________

b. ______________________________

c. ______________________________

d ______________________________

e. ______________________________

f. ______________________________

5. Joel says, "I didn't like undressing with the guys in the showers. They had more pubic hair than I did."

a. ______________________________

b. ______________________________

c. ______________________________

6. Phyllis says, "I couldn't wait for it [my period] to start."

a. ______________________________

b. ______________________________

c. ______________________________

d ______________________________

e. ______________________________

UNIT 16
PARENTAL INFORMATION

What guesses might you make given the following data?

1. Father is 62 and mother is 40. They have been married for 20 years.

   a. ______________________________

   b. ______________________________

   c. ______________________________

2. Mother is 43 and father is 54. They have been married 12 years. Their only child, Sol, is 4 years old.

   a. ______________________________

   ____

   b. ______________________________

   ____

   c. ______________________________

   ____

   d. ______________________________

   ____

   e. ______________________________

   ____

   f. ______________________________

   ____

   g. ______________________________

   ____

3. Maury's and Sharon's father was a surgeon. He was gone all the time. [Make inferences about father, mother, and the children.]

   a. ______________________________

   ____

   b. ______________________________

   ____

c. ______________________________

____

d. ______________________________

____

e. ______________________________

____

f. ______________________________

____

g. ______________________________

____

h. ______________________________

____

i. ______________________________

____

j. ______________________________

____

k. ______________________________

____

l. ______________________________

____

m. ______________________________

____

4. Alfred's father was a salesman. He was on the road 4-5 days a week. He slept much of the time when he was home.

   a. ______________________________
   b. ______________________________
   c. ______________________________
   d. ______________________________
   e. ______________________________
   f. ______________________________

5. Brenda's mother was a schoolteacher.
   a. ____________________

   ____
   b. ____________________

   ____
   c. ____________________

   ____
   d. ____________________

   ____

6. Miriam's father was a lawyer. Her mother was an English professor.
   a. ____________________

   ____
   b. ____________________

   ____
   c. ____________________

   ____
   d. ____________________

   ____
   e. ____________________

   ____

7. Estelle was father's favorite because she got good grades in school.
   a. ____________________
   b. ____________________
   c. ____________________

8. Mother favored Frederick because he was a boy.
   a. ____________________
   b. ____________________

9. Eric claimed that both parents favored his older brother.

a. ______________________________

b. ______________________________

c. ______________________________

d. ______________________________

e. ______________________________

f. ______________________________

g. ______________________________

h. ______________________________

i. ______________________________

10. Oscar was favored by father and seemed to be most like him.

a. ______________________________

b. ______________________________

c. ______________________________

11. Willard's parents were content if he merely passed in school.

a. ______________________________

____

b. ______________________________

____

c. ______________________________

____

d. ______________________________

____

e. ______________________________

____

12. Carol's parents "would only be pleased if I were tops."

a. ______________________________

____

b. ______________________________

____

c. ______________________________

____

d. ______________________________

____

e. ______________________________

____

f. ______________________________

____

g. ______________________________

____

h. ______________________________

____

i. ______________________________

____

13. Kay "wasn't aware of any ambitions my parents had for me."

a. ______________________________

____

b. ______________________________

____

c. ______________________________

____

d. ______________________________

____

14. Their parents wanted Mark to be a professional and Nancy to be a wife and mother.

a. ______________________________

____

b. ______________________________

____

c. ______________________________

____

d. ______________________________

____

15. Gary was told, "Be anything you want but don't take after your father."

a. ______________________________

____

b. ______________________________

____

c. ______________________________

____

16. Ben claims, "I could never confide in my father."

a. ______________________________

b. ______________________________

c. ______________________________

d. ______________________________

e. ______________________________

f. ______________________________

g. ______________________________

17. Natalie's parents were demonstrative with affection.

a. ______________________________

____

b. ______________________________

____

c. ______________________________

____

d. ______________________________

____

18. Lou's father died when Lou was 3 years old.

a. ______________________________

b. ______________________________

c. ______________________________

d. ______________________________

e. ______________________________

f. ______________________________

g. ______________________________

h. ______________________________

i. ______________________________

j. ______________________________

k. ______________________________

19. Sylvia reports that her parents hardly ever fought.

a. ______________________________

____

b. ______________________________

____

c. ______________________________

____

d. ______________________________

____

e. ______________________________

____

20. Marcy says her parents fought all the time.

a. ______________________________

____

b. ______________________________

____

c. ______________________________

____

d. ______________________________

____

e. ______________________________

____

f. ______________________________

____

g. ______________________________

____

h. ______________________________

____

21. Laurie is 24 years old. Her mother is 32 and her father is 40.

a. ______________________________

b. ______________________________

c. ______________________________

d. ______________________________

UNIT 17
OTHER FAMILY INFORMATION

What conclusions might you draw from the following information?

1. Leonard grew up in a poor family. He couldn't afford the things his friends bought.

   a. ____
   b. ____
   c. ____
   d. ____
   e. ____
   f. ____
   g. ____
   h. ____
   i. ____

2. Betsy grew up in one of the wealthiest families in the neighborhood. Others looked up to and envied her family.

   a. ____
   b. ____
   c. ____
   d. ____
   e. ____
   f. ____
   g. ____
   h. ____

3. Harvey says his neighbors thought his family was strange.

   a. ____
   b. ____
   c. ____
   d. ____
   e. ____

4. Stan reported, "We were the only Jews in the neighborhood."

a. ______________________________

b. ______________________________

c. ______________________________

d. ______________________________

e. ______________________________

f. ______________________________

g. ______________________________

5. Keith's father was an Irish Catholic and his mother was an Italian Catholic.

a. ______________________________

b. ______________________________

c. ______________________________

d. ______________________________

6. Mickey's father was Russian Orthodox and his mother was Methodist.

a. ______________________________

b. ______________________________

c. ______________________________

d. ______________________________

7. Pearl was a scrupulous* Catholic as a child.

a. ______________________________

b. ______________________________

c. ______________________________

d. ______________________________

e. ______________________________

f. ______________________________

g. ______________________________

* "Scrupulous" is defined as the tendency to see sin where none exists and to magnify the sin where it does exist

UNIT 18
EARLY RECOLLECTIONS – MANNER OF RESPONSE

What are some possible conclusions you might draw from the following situations?

1. In collecting early recollections from Esther, she says, "I can't remember anything."

   a. ____

   ____

   b. ____

   ____

   c. ____

   ____

   d. ____

   ____

2. Saul says, "I always used to go with my father for Sunday walks. I loved the time we had together, just he and I."

   ____

   ____

3. Diane says, "I can't visualize it, but I know it happened. My parents always tell the story of when I tried to stick my sister's toes with a fork when I was two years old."

   ____

   ____

4. Alan gives you a childhood dream.

   ____

   ____

5. Brian says, "I'm not sure whether I remember this or whether I've heard this story so often that I think I remember this."

   ____

   ____

6. Diana says, "We used to go to the movies every Saturday. One Saturday I saw 'Frankenstein'. I was so scared on the way home because I thought the monster might be following me."

    ____

    ____

7. Betsy tells you a recurrent dream.

    ____

    ____

UNIT 19
EARLY RECOLLECTIONS – TYPOLOGICAL APPROACH

1. **Age 2-3:** My parents gave me a toy piano. I was delighted.
   Type:________________________

2. **Age 6:** It was the first day of first grade. I went home at noon and told my mother that I wasn't going back.
   Type:________________________

3. **Age 6-7:** My younger brother and I were both on the sundeck. We were going to jump off. We counted to three and I jumped and my brother stayed. I hit the ground in a squatting position and couldn't straighten out. I walked in a squat for half an hour. It just hurt.
   Type:________________________

4. **Age 2-3:** I was lying in the crib, unable to move. I couldn't get up. I screamed. Mother rushed upstairs, picked me up and told me everything was okay.
   Type:________________________

   Type:________________________

5. **Age 4:** My mother dressed me in long underwear. I didn't like it. I went to the window, held onto the handles, and crapped my pants.
   Type:________________________

6. **Age 6 months:** I was on a train. I looked out the window and saw a headless horse running with blood coming out of his neck.
   Type:________________________

7. **Age 7:** I was told to sit on the porch. Children were throwing rocks. I stood up and got hit.
   Type:________________________

8. **Age 7-8:** I was at camp. The nurse wouldn't let me go in the water because of an allergy. I was upset.
   Type:________________________

9. **Age 8:** I was madly in love with a girl. I was at her house. The family was eating breakfast. They were giggling. Later I discovered my fly was open. I was mortified.
   Type:________________________

10. **Age 5-6:** I was left alone in the house, waiting for my mother to return. I threw up and then was frightened she would punish me.
Type:________________________

11. **Age 4:** I came into the room dancing. I fell and sprained my ankle while twisting.
Type:________________________

12. **Age 4:** One day a boy invited me to sit on the doorstep with him. I didn't want to wrinkle my dress. He offered me three-quarters of the step. I refused. I said, "If you're my boyfriend, you ought to give me the whole step." He did. I sat down and spread out my dress.
Type:________________________

13. **Age 4:** My mother sent me to the store with a dollar. She warned me about bringing home change. I bought bubble gum. Mother asked for the change. I wouldn't tell her what I did with it. Mother beat me with the leather strap and put me to bed. I was angry with mother, hated her for the harshness of the beating.
Type:________________________

14. **Age 6:** I was playing with a Santa Claus house on the floor. A male cousin stepped on it. I don't recall what happened later or my feelings.
Type:________________________

15. **Age 7:** I got an Indian costume for Christmas. Children gathered from the whole neighborhood to get a picture taken. All the kids admired the costume. I was proud that I was the only one to have an Indian costume.
Type:________________________

16. **Age 5:** I caught diphtheria and was quarantined. Father brought me a chocolate bar. He passed it through the window. I was thrilled.
Type:________________________

17. **Age 3:** I was in a playpen in a covered back porch. A leaf was floating on the porch. I thought it was a bee. I was terrified and I screamed. Mother was busy in the house. She finally came out, caught the leaf and showed it to me. This pacified me but then mother dropped it. It began floating again and I began to scream.
Type:________________________

18. **Age 5:** I sat in the skating rink while my brother skated. My brother met a girl and because of this, we got home at 5:10 instead of 5:00 p.m. Father came after us with a belt. My brother ran around the table; I ran under it. We were caught.
Type:________________________

19. **Age 5:** Mother was getting ready to go out and hired a sitter. I didn't want a sitter so I cut up mother's formal with scissors. Mother was very upset but put on another dress and went. I felt remorseful.
Type:________________________

20. **Age 1 ½:** I was very small and could walk, but mother still nursed me. At Grandma's house I got a little stool, pushed it over to mother and asked her to nurse me. She did.
Type:________________________

21. **Age 6:** It was the first day of first grade in a new school. I knew the first grade teacher had been my kindergarten teacher. I thought I was in kindergarten. I told the teacher since I was worried. The teacher reassured me and yelled at me.
Type:________________________

22. **Age 6:** A kids' show was on T.V. and all the kids were supposed to be eating their lunch. I spilled my food and asked my brother to cover the T.V. so Uncle Johnny (T.V. host) wouldn't see. When he said, "Did you eat it all?" I said, "Yes." I lied. I felt that at least he wouldn't holler at me. I was safe. He wouldn't find out.
Type:________________________

23. **Age 3-4:** I was in the living room. I was sitting on my uncle's lap. My father was sitting next to us on the floor. I was running a train set. I was happy, enjoying myself.
Type:________________________

24. **Age 6:** I was in first grade. I was doing private reading. A boy was picked by the teacher to help others with words they didn't know. I picked a word which I knew but asked him anyway. He didn't know the word and went to ask teacher. I called him back and told him I really knew it. I felt guilty.
Type:________________________

25. **Age 4:** My brother bragged. Father told him he mustn't brag. I resolved I wouldn't be caught bragging.
Type:________________________

26. **Age 5:** We were practicing singing for an assembly. I yawned. Teacher rebuked me. I felt she was unfair since I thought a yawn was uncontrollable, like a sneeze.
Type:________________________

27. **Age 5:** I was in kindergarten. The teacher was showing us how to draw. I thought her drawing was nice. It was much better than I could do.
Type:________________________

28. **Age 3-4:** I was carrying a stick, fell on the stairs and cut myself.
Type:________________________

29. **Age 8-9:** The space shuttle flew over our house. I just observed it. I had no feelings about it.
    Type:_______________________

30. **Age 8:** I wanted to build something. I asked the landlord for something. The landlord went ahead and built it for me. I felt disappointed.
    Type:_______________________

31. **Age 5:** I visited school before going to school myself. Mother had made me a beret. As we filed into our school, the principal lifted my beret by the tassel. I was infuriated and spanked him. He thought it was amusing.
    Type:_______________________

32. **Age 5:** I went picking strawberries with a new dress on. It got stained. I dabbed it with cold water. Mother saw me and told me I could have gotten the stains out better with warm water.
    Type:_______________________

    Type:_______________________

33. **Age 7:** My parents were getting married in church. Father had a grey suit, mother had a navy blue dress with red flowers and a corsage. I was sitting in a pew with grandmother. I was wearing a gold corduroy skirt and vest and a flower I don't recall any feelings.
    Type:_______________________

    Type:_______________________

34. **Age 9:** I was the last one standing in the spelling bee. I was proud. It felt good.
    Type:_______________________

35. **Age 7-8:** Older boys were expert kite makers. A friend and I decided to make a kite which could stay out all night. Others had tried and failed. We were going to build successful one. Other fellows laughed at us. I'm not sure whether out kite stayed up or not.
    Type:_______________________

36. **Age 4:** I had a train on the back porch. I pushed the train around the track.
    Type:_______________________

37. **Age 5:** in kindergarten the girl who sat in front of me wet her pants. I laughed at it.
    Type:_______________________

UNIT 20
EARLY RECOLLECTIONS – HEADLINE TECHNIQUE

Write a headline for each of the following ERs.

Your headline should include an action verb.

Example:

Male
Age 4-5: I stopped a man in the street. I told him another boy wanted to hurt me. I don't recall what else happened.
Headline: *Boy seeks help from a man.*

---

1. **Jennifer**
   Age 6: At my birthday party. I was sitting on the back porch with a boy who had brought me a dozen roses.

Headline:____

2. **Jose**
   Age 3-4: Mother was doing the washing in the kitchen. I was riding around on my little red kiddy-car over the dirty clothes. I was thinking how terrible it was that mother had to work so hard.

Headline:____

3. **Mary**
   Age 3: My aunt and I were sitting and reading. All of a sudden I swooped off to my great aunt's house. When I returned, my brother was ill. It was a little baffling because I had never seen my brother ill.

Headline:____

4. **Joe**
   Age 4-5: A neighbor had a goat and wagon. I raised hell because I wanted the goat and wagon. I screamed and yelled. Felt cheated.

Headline:____

5. **Jerome**
   Age 6-7: There was a parade with a man in an open car; excitement in the crowd. I didn't understand what it was all about but felt caught up in the excitement.

Headline:____

6. **Nikona**
   Age 2-3: I ate brown baby food. It was real. My mother was feeding me. I felt happy.

Headline:____

7. **Ronald**
   Age 4: My parents went out at night. I was sleeping in the same room with my sister. I thought I heard a voice saying, "Aha." I was frightened and got into bed with my sister.

Headline:____

8. **Mark**
   Age 4: A dog was chasing me. It looked mad. It finally gave up. But it scared the life out of me.

Headline:____

9. **Vern**
   Age 4: A puppy came in my direction. I ran and fell and hit the corner of the step and cut myself. I was bleeding like a pig and ran into the house screaming. Father and mother took care of me. Mother quieted me down.

Headline:____

10. **Alicia**
    Age 4: I was at Sunday School. Everyone was saying prayers. I put my hands over my ears. The teacher rebuked me. I felt mortified.

Headline:____

11. **Monique**
    Age 7: My parents were arguing. I came out of another room, looked around, asked if they'd lower their voices and returned to my room.

Headline:____

12. **Lawrence**
    Age 8: A boy attacked me as I left school. I hated fighting. I got him down and made him promise to leave me alone.

Headline:____

13. Francine

Age 8: The teacher asked something. I answered "internal dissension." The teacher asked where I'd learned that. I was proud of it.

Headline:____

14. Robert

Age 5: One day I was kidded by some adult relatives for liking a girl. It hurt.

Headline:____

15. Maria

Age 3: I was sitting on the back porch with grandmother. A storm came up. We pulled the furniture inside. We made it just in time. The storm blew the screens down.

Headline:____

16. Wendy

Age 3: Mother took me uptown for a walk. Mother had dressed me up. Had good feelings.

Headline:____

17. Crystal

Age 4: It was the 4th of July at night at an amusement park. I was with my parents. I didn't like the loud noises and cried. They explained to me about the fireworks and comforted me.

Headline:____

18. Noah

Age 5-6: Father told me not to play in the garage. I did, and I fell down and cut open both knees.

Headline:____

19. Michelle

Age 5-6: Three kids threw rocks at me. I ran home and told mother. Another girl and I came back and beat those three kids.

Headline:____

20. Orla

Age 5: It was Christmas time. I had on a new coat and hat. A street photographer photographed me on a pony with Santa Claus standing next to me. I enjoyed it.

Headline:____

21. George

Age 5: I smoked one of father's cigarettes under a neighbor's porch. I got sick, moaned and groaned. Mother found me and gave me a beating.

Headline:____

UNIT 21
EARLY RECOLLECTIONS – SELF CONCEPT

Write a self concept for the following ERs.

1. **Age 3:** I climbed to the top of the bureau. I found a razor blade there. I fell off and cut my nose.

   When I____

2. **Age 4-5:** Another boy and I were talking about hair. He had black hair and I had brown. Black hair was more masculine.

   I am____

3. **Age 7-8:** My parents took me along for the walks. This day there wasn't enough room on the sidewalk. They urged me to walk ahead or behind. I felt left out.

   I am____

   I am____

4. **Age 4:** I pushed a red wagon up a hill. I felt good. Felt independent.

   When I____

   When I____

5. **Age 7-8:** A boy tried to beat me up. I was scared and resigned myself to being beaten up. I didn't fight back. I rationalized, "If I weren't a cripple (I had club feet), I could beat him."

   I am____

   I am____

   When I feel ________________________, I ____________

   ____

6. **Age 8:** My brother and a friend and I got into trouble at school. We were sent into the cloakroom where we ate all the lunches. The teacher hit us. It hurt. Eating the lunches was my idea because I wanted to get even with the teacher.

   I am____

   I am____

7. **Age 8-9:** In the country. I climbed a big tree and threw rocks at the caretaker of the cottage down below. I had no fear whatsoever. I felt like nothing could happen to me.

   I am____

   I am____

8. **Age 5:** First day of school. I was very nervous at the thought of going to school. When mother came after school to get me, I was very glad it was over.

   I am ____

   I am relieved when____________________________________

9. **Age 6:** First day of school. I went with mother. Felt overwhelmed. Kids were glancing at me with hostile expressions. Was upset. I didn't like the thought of mother leaving. Felt kind of lost.

   I feel____

10. **Age 7:** Riding on a bus with family. Father was to stay on, the others to get off. I stayed on. Father tried to put me off to catch up with the family myself. I felt panicky. Father took me along.

    I am____

    I need____

    I do____

UNIT 22
EARLY RECOLLECTIONS – SELF IDEAL

Write a self ideal conviction for the following ERs.

1. **Age 5:** Went on trip. There was a platform on a tree. My sister and I climbed up on the platform. It gave me tremendous pleasure. I was higher than my parents.

In order to have a place, I should

____

____

2. **Age 5-6:** I went to a farm with my uncles and mother and father. My uncles got into the pig sty and began to kick the pigs. I tried the same thing. It was a lot of fun.

In order to have a place, I should

____

____

3. **Age 5:** I was stacking pies and pretending to be a businessman taking orders on the phone.

In order to have a place, I should

____

____

4. **Age 5:** Having my picture taken by a photographer. Had on my favorite dress. I had to sit on the kitchen table on top of a catalogue so that my dress was out in front of me. He took my picture. I felt pretty sitting up on the catalogue, being elevated, and I had on my pretty dress.

In order to have a place I should ____

In order to have a place I should ____

In order to have a place I should ____

5. **Age 5-6:** Mother asked my cousin to carry me on his shoulders in the country because I was the baby and it was a long walk. I felt good that I could be carried and didn't have to walk.

In order to have a place, I should ______________________________

(and) I should ______________________________

6. **Age 8-9:** One day I was picked by the teacher to perform a special service. I liked it.

In order to have a place, I should

____

____

7. **Age 4:** Went to train station to see trains. Father lifted me into the engineer's cab. It was dark inside. Had good feelings.

In order to have a place, I should

____

____

8. **Age 4:** Mother wanted me to eat lettuce. I wouldn't and didn't.

In order to have a place, I should

____

____

9. **Age 3:** I burned my hand. I recall then sitting on the couch. Father wrapped my hand in a handkerchief. I felt safe and good because all four of us were together.

In order to have a place,______________________________

In order to have a place,______________________________

10. **Age 9:** I got off a bus and ran in front of it. A car almost hit me.

If I'm not______________________________

____

UNIT 23
EARLY RECOLLECTIONS – *WELTBILD*

Write your conclusions for the following ERs:

1. **Age 6:** I played truant one day. The next day the principal came and slapped my hand.

If I do wrong, people ____

2. **Age 7:** I was standing behind a swing awaiting my turn. A boy swung back and knocked my tooth loose.

Life is____

3. **Age 5:** The first day of school. The teacher was very nice. She gave us treats to eat. There were pillows to lie on. I enjoyed it.

Life is____

Women____

4. **Age 5:** Competitive game at school, boys versus girls. The teacher went out of the room when she came back, she immediately awarded victory to the girls. I thought it was unfair.

Women____

5. **Age 8:** I bet a boy (roller skates vs. a BB gun) that I could jump four stairs. I won the bet and took his gun home. My parents wouldn't let me keep it. I thought it was unfair because I had won it fair and square.

People are____

6. **Age 4:** I walked to the baseball field at the pitcher's box. They didn't see me since I was small. I got hit by the bat.

Little people____

7. **Age 5:** My grandmother was on the porch swing and I had my head in her lap. I felt secure and comfortable.

People (or women) are here to____________________________________

8. **Age 5:** I woke up thinking lions were roaring in the zoo. Actually my father was snoring. I cried. Mother came in and comforted me. I felt relieved and went to sleep.

Men____

Women____

9. **Age 5-6:** I hit a girl in the eye with a snowball accidentally. I ran away and hid in the basement. My mother found me and promised not to punish me. When I came out, she gave me the spanking of my life.

Women____

10. **Age 5:** First day of kindergarten. I was sitting in a room with kids in a circle. They were crying. I didn't know what they were crying about.

Life is____

11. **Age 7-8:** Fight on the street. One man had a gun, one had a knife. They were walking toward each other. I was standing on the curb, watching. I was scared.

The world of men centers about____

12. **Age 5:** I was in the park with my siblings and mother. My brother had a temper tantrum. I was embarrassed. I felt sorry for mother since she couldn't handle him. I felt angry with my brother.

Other people are____

Women____

13. **Age 7:** My grandmother lived on a hill. Father parked the car. My brother and I climbed into the car and kicked off the brake. The car rolled back and hit another car. Mother had a fit and made us stay in the yard the next day.

Men___________________________, and women___________________________

14. **Age 5:** Visiting my aunt's house in a poor neighborhood. Someone sent me to the corner store. Was very dark. Was scared. On the way back a grown man was following me. I couldn't run fast enough. Scared shitless.

Life is____

Men are ____

15. **Age 7-8:** I had to go to the bathroom very badly. My sister was in there. I busted in. She was sitting on the toilet. I urinated on her. I don't recall any feelings at the time.

Women are____

Women's needs are ____

UNIT 24
EARLY RECOLLECTIONS – ETHICAL CONVICTIONS

Write your conclusions for the following ERs.

1. **Age 8:** I did something wrong in school. The teacher sent me to the principal who asked my mother to come in. I felt very ashamed.

If I do something wrong,____

2. **Age 4:** A girl and I were caught under the bed playing doctor. Mother said, "Naughty," and told us not to do that again.

It is wrong____

Women are____

3. **Age 8:** My uncle gave me a knife and I lost it. My parents asked me what happened to the knife. I said I left it in school. Later they discovered the loss and they were angry because I lied. My father threatened to spank me.

Honesty____

4. **Age 5:** Putting on a vest with an elastic. Elastic slipped. Button hit the nanny who spanked me and took my toys away.

If I do wrong, ____

One false move and ____

5. **Age 7-8:** Caught in a lie, mother asked if I'd taken some candy. Mother spanked me. I cried.

Lying ____

Women ____

6. Under 5 years: Came into the room. Sister was trying on a white dress. Someone told me not to mess sister's dress. I deliberately spilled juice on it. Was punished.

Mischief ____

If something is prohibited______________________________________

7. **Age 4-5:** Mother was ill in bed. I pooped on the floor just to be ornery since I knew mother couldn't get out of bed to punish me.

I do wrong then____

8. **Age 4:** Cousins visiting. I was disgusted since one of the cousins chewed potatoes with his mouth wide open. Was almost shocking.

People who do wrong____

I am the____

9. **Age 6:** At my aunt and uncle's home. They had a girl, 4 or 5 years old. They were going to take both kids to Kiddieland. Uncle threatened to not take me if he found my sucking my thumb. When he returned to the room, I was sucking my thumb. He yelled at me and told me I couldn't go. I cried, ran to my aunt who said if I'd be good, I could go. I went.

Being good____

Being bad____

When one does wrong, one can____________________________________

Men are ____

I am technically correct even though________________________________

____

10. **Age 5:** I had an "A" in conduct on my report card. My mother told me that was good and gave me a dollar.

Good behavior ____

UNIT 25
EARLY RECOLLECTIONS – SEQUENTIAL ANALYSIS (TYPES)

1. Example:

a. **Age 9:** We had a spelling bee. I was the last one standing. It felt great.

b. **Age 7:** We were at a picnic and they had races for prizes. I came in second in my heat. I was crushed.

c. **Age 8:** We were playing "king of the mountain". While everybody was pushing everyone around to get to the top, I sneaked around the other side and walked up to the top unmolested. I don't' recall how long I stayed on top but it sure felt good being there.

d. **Age 7:** It was the first day of school. All the kids were crying. I felt it was silly of them.

Type: ____________________

2. Example:

a. **Age 3:** One time I made in my pants. I was playing in the yard. Felt ashamed.

b. **Age 5:** The doctor came to give me a shot every other day. One time I didn't cry. I got to be a pro at it. He was proud of me. I felt real good about being able to take a shot without screaming.

c. **Age 5:** I was riding with father to the office. I threw up in the car all over myself. I got car sick. I was very upset with myself but couldn't control it.

d. **Age 4:** I was in the hospital having my tonsils out. I didn't want to be there. Then I recall the sleeping gas. It was a black mask. It was scary. I didn't know what they would do to me. I woke up in my crib and was angry. I had to use the bedpan. The only thing they did that they said they'd do was give me ice cream. I was kicking and screaming the whole time in the hospital.

Type: ____________________

3. Example:

a. **Age 3:** We lived in Ohio. My parents gave me a toy piano. I was delighted. I played something. My parents were delighted and encouraged me.

b. **Age 4:** I ran across the street again. They lady gave me more rhubarb but grudgingly. I felt bad that I had annoyed the lady by coming over too often.

c. **Age 5:** It was the first day of school. The teacher was very nice and gave us candy. Then we all took a nap. I enjoyed it.

Type: ____________________

4. **Example:**

   a. **Age 4:** On the first day of school, I hid under my bed and said I didn't want to go. They found me and tried to drag me out. I put up a fight.

   b. **Age 6:** First grade. I wet my pants. I didn't raise my hand because I didn't have enough nerve. The teacher was very nice about it. The kids laughed. I cried. The teacher said it happens to a lot of kids. When I came home, mother spanked me. I didn't cry. I felt too belligerent and wouldn't give mother the satisfaction.

   c. **Age 4:** The kindergarten teacher said that there was to be no talking in class. I talked and the teacher sent me to the principal's office. I was mad.

Type: ____________________

5. **Example:**

   a. **Age 3:** Playing on the floor with beads. Sister (+11) picked me up and ran out to the fields to get mother. I had swallowed a bead. Mother wasn't perturbed.

   b. **Age 3:** Playing in kitchen near trapdoor. The door fell down on my leg. Sister (+11) picked me up and cried as hard as I did.

   c. **Age 3-4:** Took hold of hot poker, burned hand, screamed. Mother got a salve. I stuck my whole hand in it.

   d. **Age 7:** Nosebleed in class. I left the room. Teacher came out and petted me and took me home.

Type: ____________________

6. **Example:**

   a. **Age 3:** Lived on a corner near a gas station. Someone told us to get out of the apartment. We all went on a midway in the street. Someone was carrying me. It was just some smoking tires — nothing serious. I don't think I was very impressed. I was expecting something exiting and it was only some tires.

   b. **Age 3:** Christmas time. I had on these real pretty silk pajamas. And someone got a gift in a big box. I got in the box in my pajamas and people were taking pictures of me saying "look how cute she is." It was fantastic.

   c. **Age 7-8:** Sister and her friend took me to a science fiction movie. She said it would be scary. When the robot was knocking over things I ran to the concession stand and peered through the door. After that scene I think I went back and sat down.

Type: ____________________

UNIT 26
EARLY RECOLLECTIONS – SEQUENTIAL ANALYSIS (HEADLINES)

1. **Male**

   Age, under 2: I was in a carriage at the foot of mother's bed and someone had put a blanket over me and either in a dream (or awake), I had a vision of an old woman looking down and spitting at me. I felt scared.

   a. **Headline**: Women ______________________________

   Age 5: My tonsils were to be removed. I went to the doctor's office where there were a lot of kids. I had to change clothes and put on a type of pajamas. We played ring-around-the-rosy. I was grabbed from behind, which meant it was my turn to have my tonsils taken out. I was on a table; they were holding me down. I recall the mask. I was scared.

   b. **Headline**: Life ______________________________

   Age 6: I was in class. I wet my pants. I felt uncomfortable.

   c. **Headline**: I ______________________________

   d. **Headline**: I ______________________________

   e. **Write a summary for the above.**

   ____

   ____

   ____

   ____

   ____

   ____

2. **Female**

   Age 5: It was the first day of school. Mother took me. I was lined up with the other kids. All the mothers waited around outside. The kids marched in and we took our seats. It was my first time away from my mother. I felt happy about going to school but a little afraid since I left my mother.

   a. **Headline:**______________________________

   b. **Headline:**______________________________

Age 5: Same day. When I came home, I was happy to be home. Mother asked me how I liked school. I said that I liked it.

c. **Headline:**____

Age 7: It was my first communion. I got all dressed up in a white dress. I was excited. I went to church, marched to the altar where I received the sacrament. I was at the head of the line since I was the second shortest.

d. **Headline:**____

e. **Headline:**____

Age 7: My sisters were going to a movie. I wanted to go with them. They didn't want to take me. Mother said I couldn't go. I put up a fuss but didn't go. I felt it was unfair.

f. **Headline:**____

g. **Headline:**____

Age 6: I was a thumbsucker. Mother told me that Santa Claus would treat me good if I stopped sucking. It was Christmas morning and I found a doll and a rocking chair. I was excited about it.

h. **Headline:**____

i. **Headline:**____

Age 8: I was skating in the street. I tried to execute something fancy. I flopped, skinned my knees and ran home crying and washed my knees.

j. **Headline:**____

Age 8: We helped my teacher correct papers after school, gave them back and left. I was glad to help her. The teacher thanked us.

k. **Headline:**____

Age 6: My girl friend's uncle threw me down and tried to get on top of me. I fought with him. I was petrified; I hollered. He ran. I went home and told my mother, who had him arrested.

l. **Headline:**____

Age 6: I was in court. They asked me questions. I was frightened.

m. Headline:____

n. Write a summary for the above.

____

____

____

____

____

____

____

3. Female

Age 5: Anna, my best friend and next door neighbor, and I were going swimming. Her father, an imposing physician who frightened me because he was punitive to Ana, was driving us. I got into the front seat with him. He turned to me and asked, "Well, Sally, do you hope to get a good tanning today?" I thought, what does he mean, tanning? Tanning like a spanking or like a suntan? I don't remember saying anything, maybe mumbling. I mostly recall wondering what he meant.

a. Headline:____

Age 5-6: Anna and I were going for a picnic lunch in the woods. She had a bottle of a new kind of soda pop. Mother had packed my lunch, put it in a brown paper sack and said, "You're going to have a real (emphasized, grin on her face) treat." When we got to our picnic place, I opened my sack and my treat was Spam (yuk!) between bread. I was very disappointed and felt tricked and deceived.

b. Headline:____

c. Write a summary for the above.

____

____

____

____

____

____

____

UNIT 27
EARLY RECOLLECTIONS – SEQUENTIAL ANALYSIS
(LIFE STYLE COMPONENTS)

Write convictions for each early recollection. All components may not be present in each recollection.

BORIS

1. **Age 6:**
   I talked my little brother into drinking paint thinner while father went to the bathroom. I told my brother that father had left chocolate milk and if he wanted it, he should drink it. He did. Father returned. He asked what happened and I told him. He yelled, pointed his finger at me and said I shouldn't do it because my brother could get real sick. I think I got hit once or twice on the ass. I felt a little scared but I didn't really care one way or the other.

Self Concept:

a.____

b.____

c.____

d.____

Self Ideal:

e. ____

f. ____

g. ____

***Weltbild*:**

h. ____

i. ____

Ethical Convictions:

j.____

2. **Age 7:**
   In our new house my brother was coming downstairs with a juice glass. He slipped on the gray stairs. He dropped the glass and cut his hand. I started laughing at him and then went and told grandmother. They took him to the hospital and I had to stay with a neighbor. It didn't bother me. It was him, not me.

Self Concept:

a.____

b.____

Self Ideal:

c.____

***Weltbild*:**

d.____

e.____

f.____

3. **Age 8:**
   I fell off my bike at high speed on gravel. I tore up both my legs and my new pants. I could hardly walk home. The bike was bent up. I thought I'd really get it from father. At home father cleaned the wounds. When mother came home and saw me, she yelled at father for not having taken me to the hospital. Father said, "He'll live." I was upset that neither of them took me to the hospital. I felt like they didn't care.

Self Concept:

a.____

b.____

Self Ideal:

c.____

***Weltbild*:**

d.____

e.____

f.____

4. Age 7:
It was my first day in my new school. It was in second grade. I was scared. There were new kids and I wasn't used to it. The old school had older teachers. This place had real young ones. I was sitting in class. I didn't know anyone except the teacher. I felt kind of safe with the teacher because I'd met her the day before. It felt kind of scary with the kids because I didn't know any of them.

Self Concept:

a.____

b.____

Self Ideal:

c.____

***Weltbild*:**

d.____

e.____

5. Age 8:
I ran out into the street. A driver came flying down the street and knocked me about 10 or 15 feet. I got up and walked away. He screamed, "I hit you!" and then he told my grandmother who said, "If the boy's all right, then don't worry about it." I didn't care. I was all right and just wanted to go play.

Self Concept:

a.____

b.____

c.____

Self Ideal:

d.____

***Weltbild*:**

e.____

f.____

Write a summary statement of the above convictions.

____

____

____

____

____

____

____

____

ORVILLE

1. Age 3-4:

It was voting day. They glued billboard signs on the sidewalk. I saw them from the window and then I went downstairs. I couldn't believe it – all of a sudden the neighborhood was transformed. What I really wanted to know was how they would get that off the sidewalk. Someone told me it was about voting. I thought they said "boating". I still couldn't figure out what it was all about and how they would get it off the sidewalk.

Self Concept:

a.____

b.____

c.____

d.____

e.____

Self Ideal:

f.____

***Weltbild*:**

g.____

h.____

2. Age 3-4:

We were moving into our house. I recall my aunt falling through the air return vent. Everyone laughed. I was amazed that that could happen.

Self Concept:

a.____

b.____

***Weltbild*:**

c.____

d.____

3. Age 5:

I was sitting in class on the first day of school. Everyone was crying. I wasn't. I couldn't figure out what they were crying about.

Self Concept:

a.____

b.____

c.____

d.____

Self Ideal:

e.____

f.____

Weltbild:

g.____

4. **Age 4-5:**

I would take my mattress and slide down the stairs on it. One time I couldn't make the turn and hit the wall. I went back up and slid down again.

Self Concept:

a.____

b.____

Self Ideal:

c.____

d.____

***Weltbild*:**

e.____

5. **Age 4-5:**

I could slide through the opening between the pillar and the wall in the living room. My sister tried to do it one day and got her head stuck. She wasn't sure she could get out. My siblings tried to get her out before my parents came home. They did. I thought it was hilarious.

Self Concept:

a.____

b.____

c.____

d.____

Self Ideal:

e.____

***Weltbild*:**

f.____

6. **Age 4-5:**

My older brother was studying and my other brother took a mouse on a stick up to him. My older brother was panic-stricken and they both got into a fight. I thought the mouse part was hilarious.

Self Concept:

a.____

b. ____

***Weltbild*:**

c.____

Write a summary statement of the above convictions.

____

____

____

____

____

____

____

Made in the USA
Lexington, KY
21 May 2014